The piano pieces for CHILDREN
CHILDREN'S DREAMS
For Small Hands-No Octaves
composed by Yoshinao Nakada

こどものためのピアノ曲集
こどものゆめ
中田　喜直／作曲

edition KAWAI

ま え が き

　ピアノを正しく美しくひくためには，基礎が大切です。基礎が不十分であり，まちがったやり方であれば，まったく上達は望めません。

　こどものピアノ教育で一番困ることは，ヴァイオリンのように，小さな体，小さな手に合った楽器を使用することができないことです。大人用のヴァイオリンを，小さなこどもにひかせる先生は一人もいないのに，大きなグランドピアノをこどもにひかせて不思議に思わないのも，なんとも不思議なことです。

　そのうちに，こども用，手の小さい人のためのピアノができるはずですが（現在少しはあります）それまでは大人用の大きな重い鍵盤で，無理をしてひかなければなりませんから，手や腕を痛めたり，悪い癖がつかないように十分注意をしなければなりません。そのためには曲を選ぶことがたいせつです。バイエルなどの初心者用，初歩の曲は，オクターヴなどがありませんが，少し進歩して，ソナチネアルバム程度になりますと，オクターヴや幅広い和音などが出てきます。それを無理して指をひろげてひくと，手首や，腕に力が入って，基本的にまちがっている悪いひき方になります。そして，それを長い間続けていると，ますます悪くなってしまいます。しかし，オクターヴ以下しかない曲は，ほとんど初歩用のやさしい，音楽的にも単純な曲しかないので，小さいこどもでも，才能のある人ほど無理をして，大人の曲をひくようになります。その結果，ごくわずかな人を除き，大部分の人が悪いひき方の音のきたないピアニストになっています。

　そこで私は，こどものためのピアノ曲は，絶対にオクターヴ以下の（最高で長七度の）指のひろがりで，20年以上前から作曲してきました。そして音楽の内容は，もちろんできるだけ最高の水準を考えながらです。ですからこどものためのピアノ曲，といっても私の曲は音大を卒業したピアニストが，日本や，アメリカで演奏会や，放送などで，あるいはヨーロッパで活躍している日本の一流のピアニストが演奏しレコードに録音したりしています。このように今まで，かなり曲を書いてきましたが，この曲集は，その一番新しい作品集で，とてもやさしい曲から，かなりむずかしい曲も入っています。ですから，こどものためだけでなく，大人の人もひいていいようになっています。そして前に書いたように手首や，腕が固くならないよう，できるだけ無駄な力が入らないような自然な指使いにも注意しました（自然な正しい指使いでないと，ピアノは上達しません）。以上がこの曲集の内容の説明ですが，さらに一曲ずつの解説はこの本の後に出ていますから，それを読んで演奏の参考にしてください。なお，この本の他に，カワイ出版から赤い表紙の，私の編集した〔こどものためのピアノ小品集〕も出ていますので，合わせてお使いくだされば幸いです。

1978年5月　中 田 喜 直

Preface

The fundamentals are the most important in order to play the piano correctly and beautifully. We cannot hope for any progress if there is an inadequate or an inaccurate comprehension of the basics.

The biggest problem in teaching the piano to children is not having an appropriate sized instrument, as in teaching the violin. One has a violin to fit the size of a small body and small hands. It is a wonder that no one thinks it strange to have a small child play a large grand piano.

Before long, there will be pianos made for children and people with small hands (there are very few now), but until then, they have to strain to use a large "for -adults-only piano", and therefore, we teachers must be careful not to have our pupils impair their hands or arms or develop bad habits. Therefore, it is important to select the proper music.

There are no octaves in beginners' and rudimentary music like Beyers, but at the semi-advanced level of Sonatinen Album, there are octaves and a wide variety of chords. In order to play these pieces, one must strain to spread the fingers and force goes into the arms and wrists. This is not only bad, but also a fundamentally incorrect way to play the piano. When this is continued for a long period of time, the habit only gets worse. However, musical pieces written with less than an octave are mostly just rudimentary steps and are artistically simple. And children with ability and talent have to strain even more to play "made-for-adult pieces". As a result, with the exception of very few people, most people become pianists with very bad habits.

For this reason, I have been composing children's piano music with less than an octave (7th major interval at most), for more than 20 years. Needless to say, I have also tried to make them interesting and of the highest level artistically.

And so, my music for children has been used by graduates of music schools (academies, universities) in Japan and the United States for recitals and broadcasts; and has been performed and recorded by the best Japanese pianists active in Europe. I have written many musical pieces and this latest book includes from easy to rather difficult pieces. And so, not only children, but adults can play them. And as I have stated before, I have written them so that the player's wrists and arms do not become stiff, and without them having to use unnecessary force in the fingers. (Without correct and natural finger usuage, progress in piano playing cannot be made.)

The above is the explanation of this volume and its contents. There are detailed explanations for each piece in the book. Please read them and use them as reference in playing the peices. Furthermore, Piano Music for Children, edited by me and published by Kawai Publishing Company, can be used as a supplementary aid.

Yoshinao Nakada

May, 1978

もくじ　　　　　　　　　　　　　　　　　　　　　　　　　　　　　**CONTENTS**

1　おぎょうぎよくね……………………… 5 ……………………… On Good Behavior

2　卵のかたちの練習曲……………… 6 ……………………… Egg-shaped Drill

3　さよなら またあしたね ……………… 7 ……………………… So-long, See You Tomorrow

4　やさしい変イ長調……………… 8 ……………………… An Easy A♭ Major

5　日本のいなか……………… 9 ……………………… Japanese Countryside

6　しずかに音階はうたう……………… 10 ……………………… The Scale Sings Softly

7　冬のコラール……………… 12 ……………………… A Winter Chorale

8　冬のメロディ……………… 13 ……………………… A Winter Melody

9　おじいさんのワルツ……………… 14 ……………………… Grandfather's Waltz

10　アーモルのおじさん……………… 17 ……………………… Uncle A Minor

11　右手黒鍵……………… 18 ……………………… Right Hand, Black Keys

12　たのしいワルツ……………… 20 ……………………… The Merry Waltz

13　朝のさんぽ……………… 22 ……………………… A Morning Walk

14 元気なおどり としずかなおどり ……………… 24 ……………… A Cheerful Dance, and A Quiet Dance

15　明るいひざし……………… 26 ……………………… The Bright Sunshine

16　みんなで歩こう遠くまで……………… 28 ……………………… Let's Walk Together

17　しずかなおはなし……………… 31 ……………………… A Serene Tale

18　朝のうた……………… 32 ……………………… The Morning Song

19　アルペジオ練習曲……………… 34 ……………………… Étude for Arpeggio

20 ファゴットとフリュートの対話……………… 37 ……………… A Conversation Between
The Bassoon and The Flute

21　ノクターン……………… 40 ……………………… Nocturne

22　おどりとうたと……………… 42 ……………………… A Dance and Song

23　風の即興曲……………… 45 ……………………… The Wind's Improvisation

24　演奏会用練習曲……………… 48 ……………………… Étude for Concert

練習のてびき……………… 52

53 ……………… Introduction to the Practice Lessons

表紙装幀／大西健之

3

さよなら またあしたね
So-long, See You Tomorrow

中田 喜直 作曲
Yoshinao Nakada

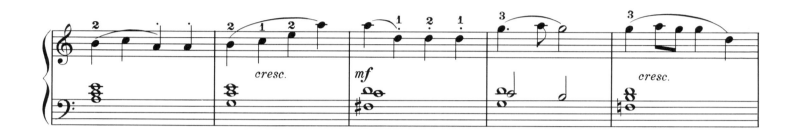
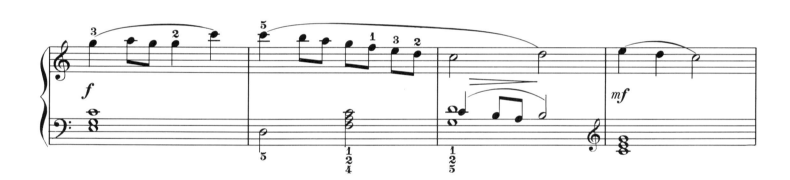
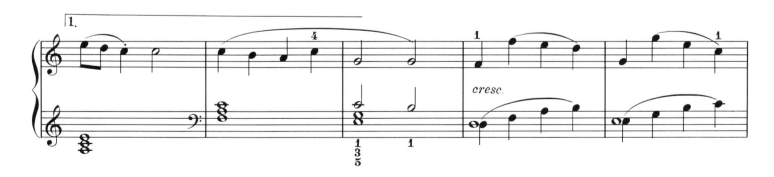
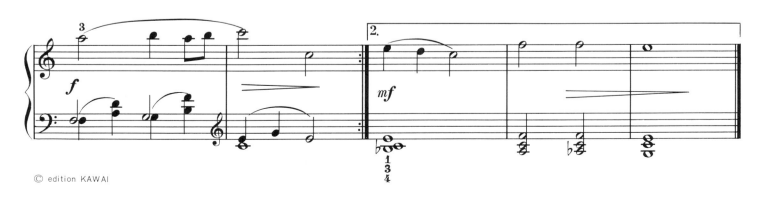

6
しずかに音階はうたう
The Scale Sings Softly

中田喜直 作曲
Yoshinao Nakada

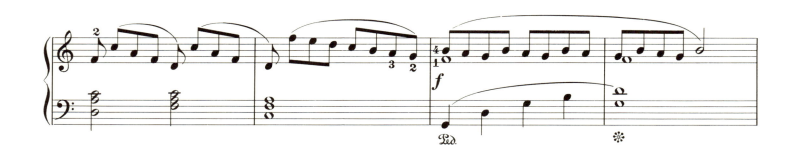

© edition KAWAI

※ この小節の左手，手の小さい人は全部 $\frac{1}{5}$ の指使いでよい。
The players with small hands can play all the left hand of this measure as $\frac{1}{5}$ fingering.

冬のコラール
A Winter Chorale

中田 喜直 作曲
Yoshinao Nakada

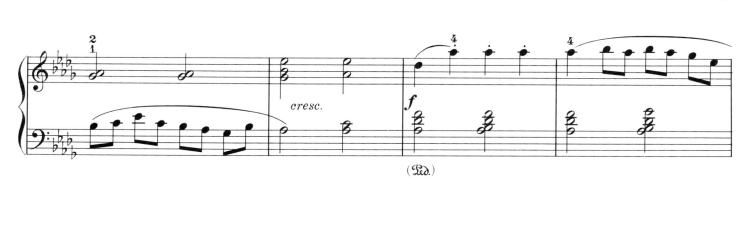

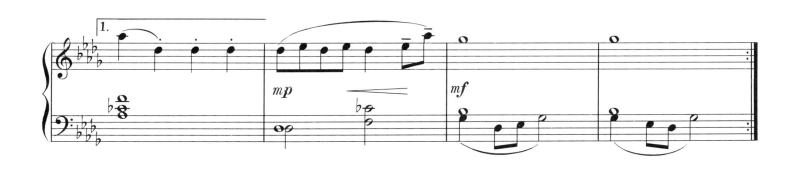

※ 右手，手がとどけば1オクターヴ下がよい。
　　Right hand: if the hands can reach the full length, play it in 8va. bassa.

21

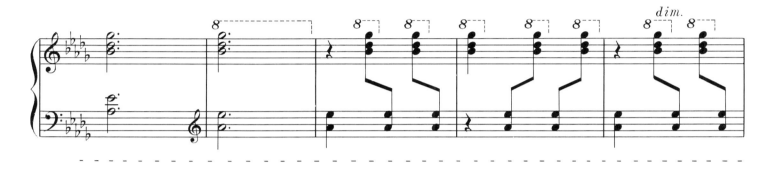
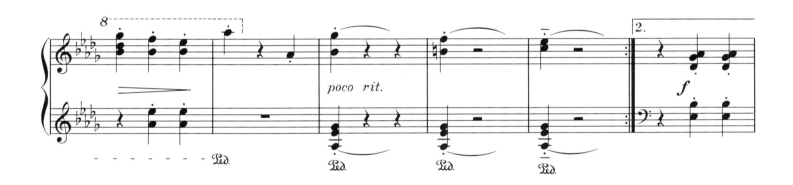

14
元気なおどり と しずかなおどり
A Cheerful Dance, and A Quiet Dance

中田 喜直 作曲
Yoshinao Nakada

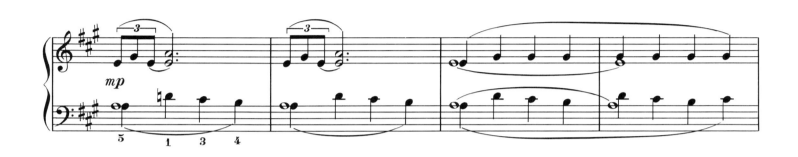
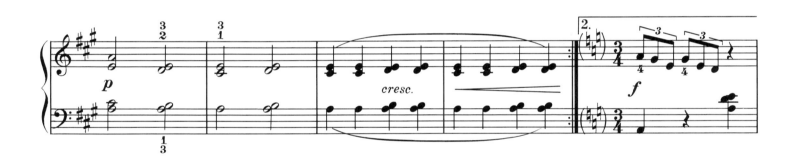

みんなで歩こう遠くまで
Let's Walk Together

中田 喜直 作曲
Yoshinao Nakada

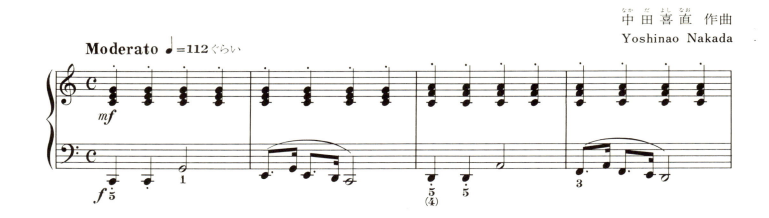

© edition KAWAI

ファゴットとフリュートの対話
A Conversation Between The Bassoon and The Flute

中田 喜直 作曲
Yoshinao Nakada

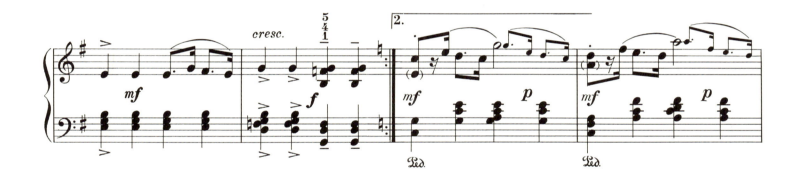
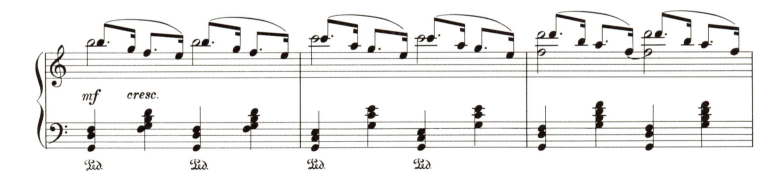
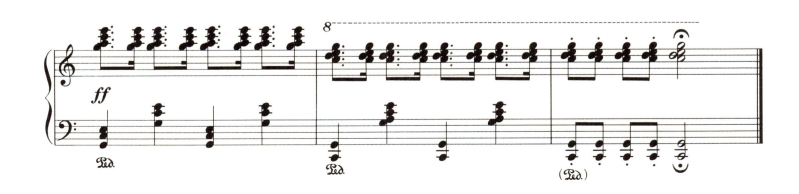

23
風の即興曲
The Wind's Improvisation

中田喜直 作曲
Yoshinao Nakada

© edition KAWAI

46

24
演奏会用練習曲
Étude for Recital

中田喜直作曲
Yoshinao Nakada

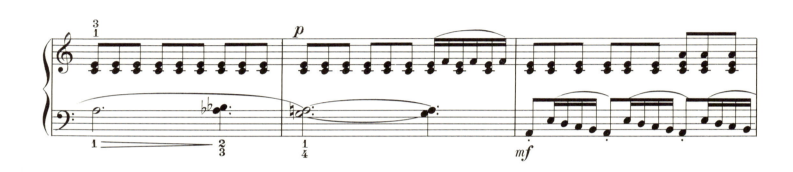

© edition KAWAI

49

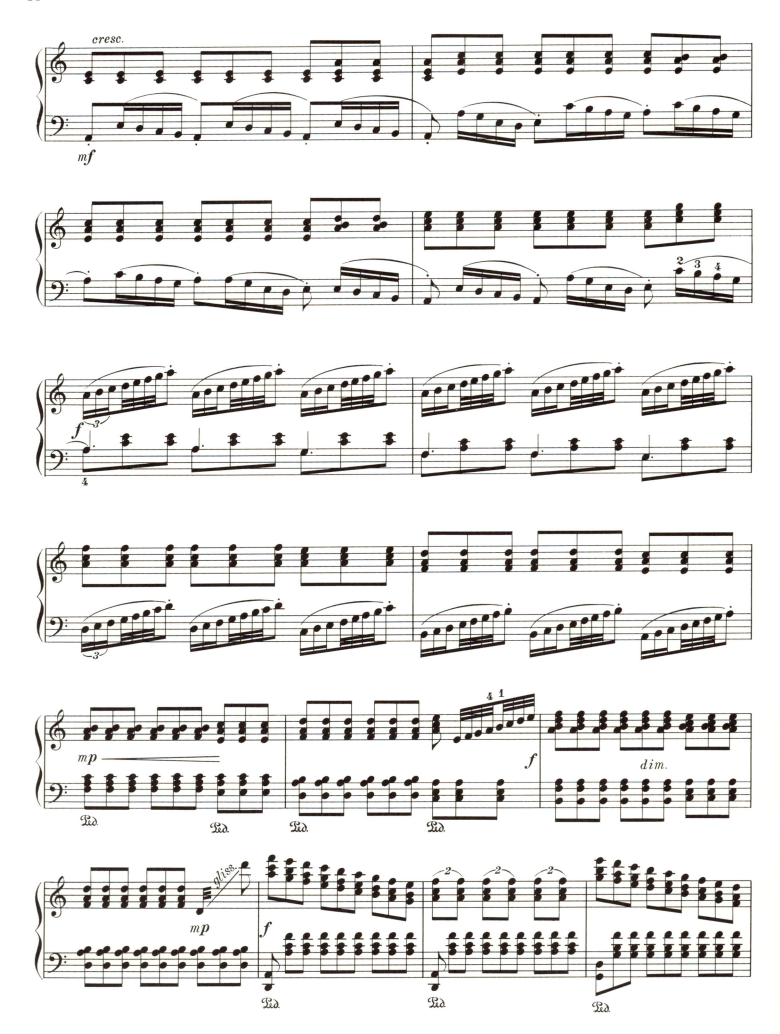

練習のてびき──中田喜直

全体を通して

指使い：なるべく小さい手を考慮してありますが、普通の手の人のことも考え、二通り書いてある部分もあります。手首や腕に力が入らないように意識して、ひきやすい方を選んでください。

ペダリング：細かく指定してありませんが、Pedの記号のある所は使用して、他の部分もそれに準じて使ってください。＊の印の所は使わない方がいい部分で、同じような所があれば、特に＊の印がなくても使わないよう考えてください。

1 おぎょうぎよくね

大部分の人は右ききであり、またピアノの練習曲も右手の訓練を主にしたものが多いので、どうしても左手が右手よりも指の動きがにぶくなります。そうすると左右そろえて音階をひくときなど左手が不正確でおくれたりして、不ぞろいになります。それでは困るので、この曲のように左手を主にした曲をまづ最初に持ってきました。指をよく上げて、特に3・4・5の指のために、よい基本の練習曲になると思います。

2 卵のかたちの練習曲

指は中指が一番長いので、ピアノをひく手の一番自然なかたちを考えると、ホ長調のドレミファソを12345の指でひくときに卵のかたちになります。♯がたくさんついていますが、この曲が一番やさしく（五本の指の位置がまったく動かないので）最初にやってもいい曲です。手をよく見ながらひいてください。

3 さよなら またあしたね

イ短調ではじまり、すぐハ長調になり、イ短調にまたもどりますが、最後はハ長調で終ります。やさしい曲ですが、ていねいにひいてください。

4 やさしい変イ長調

♭が4つついています。♭や♯がたくさんついていると、とてもむづかしいように思う人もいますが、ハ長調と音階の構造は同じです。♭が多いとなんとなく柔らかい響きがしますが、それがわかればいいと思います。

5 日本のいなか

メロディも和音も日本風、わらべうた風です。メロディが左手にも右手にも出ます。メロディをよくきかせることが必要ですが、伴奏の和音もたいせつです。最後の1小節にペダルが出てきました。

6 しずかに音階はうたう

音階風のメロディが、右手にも左手にも出てきます。題名のように、静かに歌うようにひいてください。ペダルもだいぶたくさん出てきました。ペダルがないと、響きがさびしくなる所がかなりあります。音階を美しくレガートにひく練習になります。

7 冬のコラール

和音を美しくひいてください。和音をひくとき、だいたい右手の小指の音にメロディがある場合が多いので、その音を少し他の音よりも強めにひきます。しかし、ときには内声にメロディがかくされている場合もあり、この曲では最初の2小節が右手の真中の音で、6・7小節は左手の親指にもメロディがあるのでその音を少し強く出します。和音の全部の音をただ、「べたっ」とひいたのでは音楽になりません。中級から上級まで、そのことはつねにたいせつなことです。

8 冬のメロディ

こんどは和音でなく、メロディがはっきり左右両方の手に出てきます。伴奏部はつねにメロディより弱くひかなければなりません。

9 おじいさんのワルツ

ワルツは低音をはっきり出し、2・3拍は軽く（ただし正確に）ひきます。ペダルの使い方もたいへん重要になってきます。

10 アーモルのおじさん

やさしい曲ですから、落着いて正確にひいてください。左手の小指をおさえて、他の指を動かすことは指の独立のためのいい練習になります。

11 右手黒鍵

曲名のように、右手は全部黒鍵だけ、左手も黒鍵の多い曲です。♭が6つもついていますが、やさしい曲なので、こういう曲から♭、♯の多い曲になれさせてゆきましょう。

12 たのしいワルツ

♭は5つで1つへりましたが、前の曲よりは少しむづかしい曲です。ペダルを使う所、使わない所に注意。

13　朝のさんぽ

明るくさわやかにひくことがたいせつですが，あまり調子よく早いテンポでひくと，16分音符の所がむづかしくなって，ひけなくなります。そこがちゃんとひけるテンポでひきはじめること。

14　元気なおどり と しずかなおどり

強いところはリズムも強くはっきり，4段目の弱いところはリズムもおだやかに，中間の強いところと弱いところの対照をはっきりとひいてください。

15　明るいひざし

メロディを明るく美しく，歌うようにひくこと，左手の3連符も正確に，美しい音で柔らかく。

16　みんなで歩こう遠くまで

げんきよく歩く感じでひきます。この曲も左手が右手より大きなウエイトを持っています。左手を強くするのに役立つ曲です。

17　しずかなおはなし

このへんで，少し休みたい気持で静かにひく曲です。メロディと和音の関係を考えながらひいてください。

18　朝のうた

ペダルを使ってメロディを美しく浮き上らせるようにひいてください。

19　アルペジオ練習曲

チェルニーのアルペジオの練習曲が音楽的につまらないので，

少しおもしろくしてみました。

20　ファゴットとフリュートの対話

左手のメロディはファゴット，右手はフリュート，木管楽器の低いのと高いのとの対話風です。ペダルで音を響かせるところと，ペダルを使わないところをよく区別してください。

21　ノクターン

この曲ぐらいから大人の曲といってもいいくらい，技術的にも内容的にも少しむずかしくなってきました。十分にメロディを歌い，全体の強弱，曲のまとめ方など，よく考えながらひいてください。

22　おどりとうたと

おどりの部分は，手首を柔らかく，スタッカートのひき方に注意，f・ffでもきたない音にならないように，＞の印のついているところは特にリズムに注意。歌の部分はわずかですが，十分美しく歌うように。

23　風の即興曲

3連符を流れるように美しくひき，ペダルを適当に使いながら，メロディを浮び上らせるようにします。ごつごつした感じにならぬようスマートな演奏が必要です。

24　演奏会用練習曲

指のための練習曲であると同時に，おさらい会などでひいてもはなやかにきこえるよう作った曲です。はじめはゆっくり正確にさらい，だんだん速くしてゆくこと。正確にひくことがあくまでもたいせつです。

INTRODUCTION TO THE PRACTICE LESSONS
Yoshinao Nakada

General Information

Fingers: Although the focus has been put on smaller hands, there are some pieces written with two parts, for the benefit of people with averaged-sized hands. Select the piece which is easier to play, keeping in mind not to put too much force into the arms and the wrists.
Pedaling: There are no detailed notations but do use the pedal where there are Ped. markings. Where there are (✲) markings, it is better not to use the pedal.

1. On Good Behavior
Most people are right handed and there are many piano drills made mainly for the right hand, so the fingers of the left hand become more sluggish than the right. When the scale is played with both hands the left hand falls behind in speed. That is why this piece is first. When playing it, raise the fingers high, especially the 3rd, 4th, and 5th. This is an excellent practice piece for the fingers.

2. Egg-shaped Drill
Of the fingers, the middle is the longest, and when you think of the shape of the hand in the most natural piano playing position, the 1st, 2nd, 3rd, 4th, and 5th fingers playing C D E F G in E major make the shape of an egg (or oval). There are many sharps, but this piece is the easiest (the positions of the 5 fingers do not change) and can be played first. Watch the fingers while playing.

3. So-long, See You Tomorrow

This piece begins in A minor and goes right into C major. It goes back to A minor again but ends in C major. This is an easy piece but play it carefully.

4. An Easy A♭ Major

There are 4 flats in this piece. People tend to think a musical piece is difficult when there are many flats and sharps, but the structure and the scale are the same. When there are many flats the sound is somewhat softer. It is good to understand this point.

5. Japanese Countryside

The melody and chords are Japanese WARABE-Uta style. The melody also comes out in the left hand. It is necessary to bring out the melody but the chord accompaniment is also important. The pedal is used in the last bar.

6. The Scale Sings Softly

The scale-like melody appears in both the left and the right hand. Just as the title of this piece indicates, play it as if it were softly singing. The pedal is used often. If the pedal is not used, some parts may seem incomplete. This is a practice piece for playing the scale in legato.

7. A Winter Chorale

Play the chords gracefully. When playing the chords, there is a tendency for the sound of the melody to be in the little finger of the right hand, so it is necessary to play this sound stronger than the other sounds. However, there are some parts where the melody is hidden in the inner part and in the 6th, and 7th bars, it is played with the thumb, so the sound is again a little stronger.

If the chord sounds are simply "banged," the result will not be music. This is an important point at the intermediate and advanced levels.

8. A Winter Melody

In this piece, the melody rather than the chords appear in both the left and the right hand. The accompaniment must be played more softly.

9. Grandfather's Waltz

A waltz clearly brings out the low-pitched sounds. Beats 2 and 3 are played lightly, but accurately. Using the pedal becomes important here.

10. Uncle A Minor

This is a soft piece so play it gracefully, holding down the small finger of the left hand. To move the other fingers is a good excercise for moving the fingers independently.

11. Right Hand, Black Keys

Just as the title states the right hand plays only black keys. The left hand also has many black keys to play. There are six flats, but the piece is easy. It is good to get used to playing sharps and flats with a piece like this.

12. The Merry Waltz

There are five flats in this piece. This is one less than the previous piece, but is a little more difficult. Be careful of the places where the pedal is and is not used.

13. A Morning Walk

It is important to play this piece pleasantly and refreshingly. Be careful not to get carried away and play too fast. Otherwise the 16th notes will become difficult. Begin playing at a slow tempo so that the 16th notes can be played correctly.

14. A Cheerful Dance, and A Quiet Dance

Play the strong parts clearly with power. The weak 4th line should be played gently. The weak and strong parts at the middle should be symmetrical and played clearly.

15. The Bright Sunshine

The melody should be played in a bright and song-like manner, with the triplets played accurately but softly.

16. Let's Walk Together

This is to be played in a lively beat as if walking. The left hand carries the weight in this piece. It is a good practice piece for strengthening the left hand.

17. A Serene Tale

It's time for a bit of adult music. Play this softly, keeping in mind the relation between the melody and the chords.

18. The Morning Song

Play this piece gracefully as if it floats, using the pedal.

19. Étude for Arpeggio

This is the Czerny Arpeggio practice lesson, made a little more interesting.

20. A Conversation Between The Bassoon and The Flute

The right hand melody is the bassoon and the left hand is the flute. This is a conversation-type piece using the high and low sounds of the woodwind instruments. Use the pedal to vibrate the sounds. Be sure to be able to differentiate the parts where the pedal is and is not used.

21. Nocturne

An adult piece. The music has become a little more difficult technically and artistically. Bring out the melody. Keep in mind the overall (forte and piano) loudness and softness, and the make-up of the piece.

22. A Dance and Song

Keep the wrists limp in the dance part. Be careful in playing the staccato to make sure that the sounds do not become noise in playing the f. ff., and be especially careful at the 7th sign. The song part is short but make it sing.

23. The Wind's Improvisation

Let the melody float by playing the triplets flowingly and using the pedal accordingly. It is necessary to play this piece gracefully in order not to make it rough.

24. Étude for Concert

Although this is a drill for the fingers, it can be used very well as a recital piece. Practice it slowly at the beginning and build up the tempo. It is important to play this piece accurately.

作曲者のプロフィール

● 1923年　　8月1日，東京に生まれる。
　　　　　　　父が音楽家であったため，幼少よりピアノと作曲に興味を持つ。
● 1940年　　東京音楽学校（現芸大）ピアノ科入学。
● 1943年　　9月，戦争のため，半年くり上げられ卒業，すぐ陸軍航空隊へ入る。
● 1945年　　戦争が終り復員する。
● 1947年　　このころより，作曲家として活動を始める。その後，数多くの歌曲，合
　　　　　　　唱曲，ピアノ曲，童謡，ポピュラー歌曲などを作曲し，その大部分が出
　　　　　　　版，レコード化されており，外国で演奏されることも多い。その他，放
　　　　　　　送用劇音楽，映画音楽も多く作曲した。
● 1978年　　現在，作曲活動の他，フェリス女学院大学名誉教授，（社）日本童謡協会
　　　　　　　会長などの職を勤める。
● 1949年以来，芸術祭賞はじめ，数多くの賞を受けている。
● 1986年　　紫綬褒章受章。
● 1995年　　NHK放送文化賞受章。
● 2000年　　5月3日逝去、76歳。

Biographical Sketch

1923　　Yoshinao Nakada was born on August 1. From early childhood, he had an interest in piano and composing through the influence of his musician father.

1940　　He entered the Tokyo School of Music, later renamed Tokyo University of Arts.

1943　　The war broke out in September, necessitating early graduation and enlistment in the Army Airforce.

1945　　The war ended and Nakada was discharged from military service.

1947　　From this point, he began his work as a composer. His compositions include works for the piano, children's songs, songs for chorus, and popular music. Most of his works have been published and recorded and performed in foreign countries. He has also composed music and theme songs for radio, television, and movies.

1978　　Presently, in addition to composing, Nakada also serves as the director of the Association of Children's Song Writers in Japan, and he is a professor emeritus at Ferris University.

Since 1949, Yoshinao Nakada has received many awards in music.

1986　　Nakada received the Medal with Purple Ribbon.

1995　　Nakada received NHK Broadcast Cultural Award.

2000　　Yoshinao Nakada died on May 3. Aged 76.

皆様へのお願い

　楽譜や歌詞・音楽書などの出版物を権利者に無断で複製（コピー）することは，著作権の侵害（私的利用など特別な場合を除く）にあたり，著作権法により罰せられます。
　また，出版物からの不法なコピーが行われますと，出版社は正常な出版活動が困難となり，ついには皆様方が必要とされるものも出版できなくなります。
　音楽出版社と日本音楽著作権協会（JASRAC）は，著作者の権利を守り，なおいっそう優れた作品の出版普及に全力をあげて努力してまいります。
　どうか不法コピーの防止に，皆様方のご協力をお願い申しあげます。

　　　　　　　　　　　　　　　　　カ　ワ　イ　出　版
　　　　　　　　一般社団法人　日本音楽著作権協会

		こどものためのピアノ曲集
		こどものゆめ
		作　曲●中田喜直
発行日● 1978 年 9 月 1 日　第 1 刷発行		発行所●カワイ出版　（株式会社 全音楽譜出版社 カワイ出版部）
2025 年 8 月 1 日　第 63 刷発行		〒161-0034　東京都新宿区上落合 2-13-3
		TEL.03-3227-6286　FAX.03-3227-6296
		出版情報 https://www.editionkawai.jp
		楽譜浄書●ミタニガクフ　　　写植●創美写植
英語訳●川口エレン		印刷●伸和総業株式会社・壮光舎印刷株式会社
		製本●三修紙工株式会社
		© 1978 by edition KAWAI. Assigned 2017 to Zen-On Music Co., Ltd.

本書よりの転載はお断りします。
落丁・乱丁本はお取り替え致します。
本書のデザインや仕様は予告なく変更される場合がございます。

ISBN978-4-7609-0505-8